**A Gift from the Friends of
the Scripps Ranch
Library**

THE UNIVERSE

THE SUN

ABDO
Publishing Company

A Buddy Book by Fran Howard

VISIT US AT
www.abdopublishing.com

Published by ABDO Publishing Company, 8000 West 78th Street, Edina, Minnesota 55439.

Copyright © 2008 by Abdo Consulting Group, Inc. International copyrights reserved in all countries. No part of this book may be reproduced in any form without written permission from the publisher. Buddy Books™ is a trademark and logo of ABDO Publishing Company.

Printed in the United States.

Editor: Sarah Tieck
Contributing Editor: Michael P. Goecke
Graphic Design: Maria Hosley
Cover Image: Photos.com
Interior Images: Fotosearch (page 15); Lushpix (page 17, 21, 23); NASA: (page 11); NASA: Greatest Images of NASA (page 27), JPL-Caltech (page 9), Kennedy Space Center (page 30), Marshall Space Flight Center (page 27); Photos.com (page 5, 25, 29); Stock Connection (page 29).

Library of Congress Cataloging-in-Publication Data

Howard, Fran, 1953-
  The sun / Fran Howard.
     p. cm. — (The universe)
  Includes index.
  ISBN 978-1-59928-932-8
  1. Sun—Juvenile literature. I. Title.

  QB521.5.H69 2008
  523.7--dc22
                                    2007027798

Table Of Contents

What Is The Sun?

At night, tiny lights dot the sky. These lights are stars.

Stars are glowing balls of gas that give off light. Thousands of them can be seen from Earth.

Most stars look very small and can only be seen at night. But, they are actually very large. Stars just look small because they are far away.

The sun provides light and heat for Earth. Because of this, life is able to survive on our planet.

One of the most famous stars is one we see every day. This is our sun. It is the closest star to Earth. And because the sun is so close, it appears large and bright in the daytime sky.

A Closer Look

There are many different kinds of stars. Scientists group them based on size, mass, brightness, temperature, and color.

Our sun is a dwarf star. Dwarf stars are medium-sized stars.

At the center of our sun is its core. The core is filled with gases, such as hydrogen and helium.

The surface of the sun is called the photosphere. It is much cooler than the core.

The sun's surface is surrounded by the chromosphere and the corona. These layers of gas form the sun's outer **atmosphere**. They are hotter than the sun's surface.

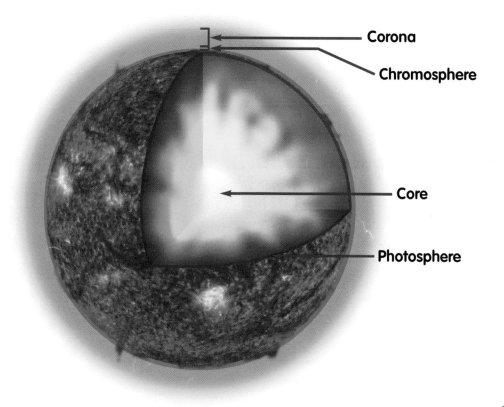

Corona

Chromosphere

Core

Photosphere

Hot! Hot! Hot!

When people think of the sun, they think of heat. The hottest part of the sun is its core. Temperatures there can reach more than 28 million degrees Fahrenheit (16 million °C)!

Stars are made of gases, such as hydrogen and helium. These gases react with each other. They get very hot and cause small **nuclear reactions**. The reactions create energy, which moves toward the surface. This causes stars to give off heat and light.

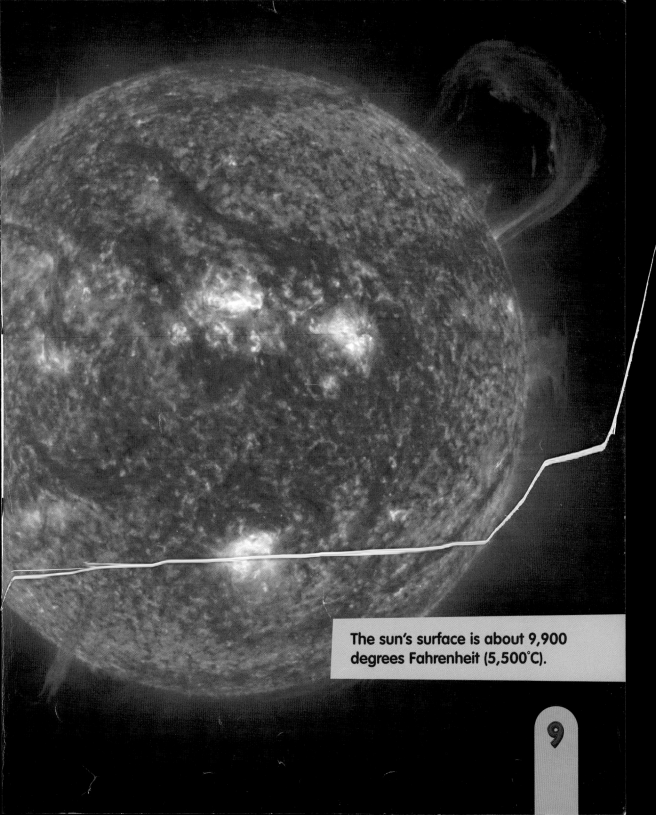

The sun's surface is about 9,900 degrees Fahrenheit (5,500°C).

9

The sun's surface, or photosphere, is very active. It is 300 miles (483 km) thick.

The photosphere is not a hard surface. Instead, the sun's hot fluids move above and below the surface. This causes the surface to have granules (GRAN-yoolz). These bumps last about ten minutes.

Large bubbles of hot gas move upward through this zone. Then, sunlight escapes into space. Sunlight provides light and heat to many planets.

Sunlight reaches Earth about eight minutes
after it leaves the sun's surface.

The Sun's Life

The sun is about 4.5 billion years old. Like other stars, it began as a cloud of gases. As a gas cloud rotates, heat and pressure begin to build. Soon, the mass begins to **collapse** on itself. At 20 million degrees Fahrenheit (11 million °C), the gas begins to burn. And after several **nuclear reactions**, a star is born!

Right now, our sun is a yellow dwarf star. Because of this scientists think it will last another 4.5 billion years.

When our sun begins to die, it will expand. Eventually, it will become a red giant star. After about 500 million years, the sun will shrink again. Then, it will become a white dwarf star and slowly cool.

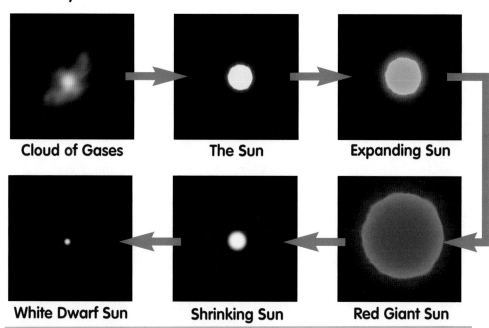

Cloud of Gases	The Sun	Expanding Sun
White Dwarf Sun	Shrinking Sun	Red Giant Sun

As stars change, there are some in-between stages. Dwarf stars grow larger as they turn into red giants. Red giants form clouds of dust and gas as they become white dwarfs.

Speed Of Light

In space, distance is measured in light-years and light-minutes. One light-year is the distance light travels in one year. This is very fast. Light travels nearly 6 trillion miles (10 trillion km) in a year!

The sun is the closest star to Earth. It is eight light-minutes away. Proxima Centauri is the second-closest star to Earth. It is about four light-years away.

Miles and kilometers are one way to measure distance on Earth. But for space, scientists need to measure distances that are far greater than distances on Earth. Light travels very fast. So, scientists found a way to use it to measure distance.

The Milky Way

Groups of stars form **galaxies**. A small galaxy has about 10 million stars. A large galaxy may have up to 1 trillion stars!

Our galaxy is called the Milky Way. It is a large galaxy. Our sun is just one of many stars in the Milky Way.

There are at least 200 billion stars in the Milky Way. Yet, only about 6,000 of them can be seen from Earth without a telescope.

Our Solar System

Our **galaxy** is filled with solar systems. A solar system is a single star with space objects, such as planets, orbiting it.

Our sun is at the center of our solar system. Earth is one of eight planets that orbit our sun. The other planets are Mercury, Venus, Mars, Jupiter, Saturn, Uranus, and Neptune.

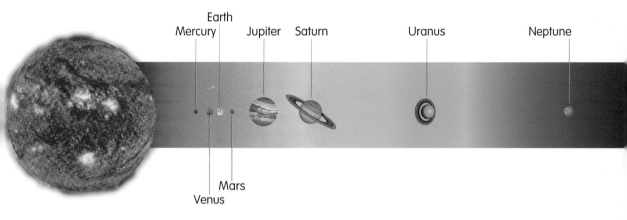

The sun provides light and heat to the entire solar system. Some planets are very hot, while others are very cold.

The sun is the only star in our solar system. But, it is one of 200 billion stars in our **galaxy**! Some scientists think our galaxy may have as many as 400 billion stars.

Our Amazing Sun

Many interesting events occur on the sun. Some of them, such as sunspots, happen on the sun's surface. These dark spots are not as hot as the surrounding areas.

The number of sunspots found on the sun changes. Sunspot activity peaks every 11 years.

The sun is also the source of solar wind. Solar wind is not like wind on Earth. It is created when energy escapes from the sun's surface and gravity.

Solar wind creates space weather. Storms in space can affect life on Earth. Space storms create the northern lights in the sky. Also, they can knock out electrical power.

The outermost layer of the **atmosphere** is called the corona. This layer is larger and hotter than the chromosphere and the photosphere.

Every so often, an explosion occurs in the sun's atmosphere. These explosions are called solar flares. Most flares occur around sunspots.

During an active period, the sun might have several solar flares each day. At other times, there may be just one in a week.

Discovering The Sun

Stars have been important to people since early times. And, people have always seen the sun. But for a long time, they didn't know that it is the center of our solar system.

In the 1500s, Polish astronomer Nicolaus Copernicus said the planets circle the sun. This was a very important discovery. Many people said this idea was wrong. But eventually, it was proven correct.

In the 1600s, Italian scientist Galileo Galilei used a telescope to study the sun. He discovered sunspots on the sun's surface.

Galileo showed people how his telescope worked.

Missions To The Sun

The first **spacecraft** to study the sun were *Pioneer 6, 7, 8,* and *9*. The United States **launched** these **probes** in the 1960s. During their orbits, scientists learned more about the sun and other stars.

In 1980, the Solar Maximum **mission** launched. It studied solar flares.

The *Solar and Heliospheric Observatory (SOHO)* **launched** in 1995. This international **spacecraft** orbits the sun. It sends a constant stream of photos to Earth.

In 1995, an *Atlas* rocket *(above)* carried *SOHO (left)* into space.

Fact Trek

Even though most stars look small from Earth, many are bigger than our sun! Giant stars can be 100 times as big as our sun and 1,000 times as bright. Supergiants are the biggest known stars in our **galaxy**.

Supergiants are the largest known stars in our galaxy.

Shadows and light make sundials work.

Long ago, people used sundials to tell time by the sun.

The sun spins around once every 27.4 days.

During a solar **eclipse**, a red rim appears around the sun.

The chromosphere and the corona are visible during solar eclipses.

Voyage To Tomorrow

People continue to explore space.
They want to learn more about the sun.
Scientists developed the Solar
Dynamics Observatory to study how
the sun affects Earth. The United States
expects to **launch** this **mission** in 2008.

The sun is too hot to get very close.
So, scientists have had to come up
with ways to learn more.

Important Words

atmosphere the layer of gases that surrounds space objects, including planets, moons, and stars.

collapse to break down.

eclipse when one space object passes in front of another, cutting off light.

galaxy a large group of stars and planets.

launch to send with force.

mission the sending of spacecraft to perform specific jobs.

nuclear reaction a change in matter that creates energy.

probe a spacecraft that attempts to gather information.

spacecraft a vehicle that travels in space.

Web Sites

To learn more about the **sun**, visit ABDO Publishing Company on the World Wide Web. Web sites about the **sun** are featured on our Book Links page. These links are routinely monitored and updated to provide the most current information available.

www.abdopublishing.com

INDEX